VALENTINE

COMPILED AND INTRODUCED BY:

STEFAN RUDNICKI

A VALENTINE

A Bouquet of
Poetry for Lovers

DOVE
BOOKS

ISBN 0-7871-1262-3

Printed in the United States of America

Dove Books
8955 Beverly Boulevard
Los Angeles, CA 90048

Distributed by Penguin USA

Cover and interior design and layout by Mauna Eichner
Cover art courtesy of The Norton Simon Foundation, Pasadena, CA
Interior illustrations by Tanya Maiboroda

First Printing: January 1997

10 9 8 7 6 5 4 3 2 1

Contents

INTRODUCTION

"Old devil time, I'm gonna fool you now . . .
When I feel low, my lovers gather round,
And help me rise to fight you one more time."
CLAUDIA SCHMIDT

THE CELEBRATION OF Valentine's Day has traditionally been associated with romantic love and the exchange, often anonymous, of gifts and greetings. Over the years, the scope of the holiday has expanded to encompass nearly every kind of relationship at every level of intimacy. Not only lovers and sweethearts, friends and family, but generations of schoolchildren, office colleagues, and others who share, however casually, time and place, have found in this special occasion an opportunity to acknowledge and celebrate a bond of love or affection with another.

All loving relationships have their cycles, and in organizing this material I have chosen an arc that will be familiar not only to lovers, but to all who love and care for one another. It is the movement of a relationship from first meeting to discovery to commitment to disappointment to renewal and ultimately to deepened faith and understanding. Each section is a variation on a theme, a movement in an orchestral fantasia that is as old and as true as life itself.

This book was originally an audio collection of love poems read by some of the most compelling personalities of our time, against a background of carefully chosen orchestral and chamber music.

The audio collection was originally a dream.

While working on a project about a murderer, I listened to dozens of hours of the recorded voice of a man who had allegedly killed two people in cold blood. It was difficult not to be affected by such material. I felt driven to understand the motives, the personality behind the deeds. Tangled in the logistics of making coherent art from life, I became engaged in a process that took on the characteristics of an obsession. I began to dream, as I do when involved in projects that defy simple solutions. I found myself in dark company both day and night, shuffling and sorting thousands of pieces of information whose only common components were violence and death.

One night, my dreaming took on a new form. The shapes and structures were similar, but the elements had changed, and I found myself arranging lines of love poetry on a canvas as vast as an open sky at dawn.

In the days that followed, I completed the murderer's story very quickly, and with great ease. Somehow, I had become disengaged.

Then I began assembling "A Valentine."

Even if most of our lives seem in some measure secure, we are without defense against the pain of others' lives, without protection from the shards of hatred and the ricochet of violence that may always be just around the corner. These affect us profoundly, especially when we feel vulnerable and alone.

Only in loving can we dispel the gloom, find a faith, become an instrument for positive change. That love may be spiritual or acutely physical. It may be the love of parents and children. It may be the comfortable affection of an old friend or the passionate hunger of a new lover. It may be the memory of a lost love, or the longing for one we have yet to find. It is all the loving in our lives together that weaves our only armor against a world gone mad.

THE FIRST DAY

John Donne

THE GOOD-MORROW

I wonder by my troth, what thou, and I
Did, till we lov'd? were we not wean'd till then?
But suck'd on countrey pleasures, childishly?
Or snorted we in the seaven sleepers den?
T'was so; But this, all pleasures fancies bee.
If ever any beauty I did see,
Which I desir'd, and got, t'was but a dreame of thee.

And now good morrow to our waking soules,
Which watch not one another out of feare;
For love, all love of other sights controules,
And makes one little roome, an every where.
Let sea-discoverers to new worlds have gone,
Let Maps to other, worlds on worlds have showne,
Let us possesse one world, each hath one, and is one.

My face in thine eye, thine in mine appeares,
And true plaine hearts doe in the faces rest,
Where can we finde two better hemispheares
Without sharpe North, without declining West?
What ever dyes, was not mixt equally;
If our two loves be one, or, thou and I
Love so alike, that none doe slacken, none can die.

THE FIRST DAY

I wish I could remember the first day,
First hour, first moment of your meeting me;
If bright or dim the season, it might be
Summer or winter for aught I can say.
So unrecorded did it slip away,
So blind was I to see and to foresee,
So dull to mark the budding of my tree
That would not blossom yet for many a May.
If only I could recollect it! Such
A day of days! I let it come and go
As traceless as a thaw of bygone snow.
It seemed to mean so little, meant so much!
If only now I could recall that touch,
First touch of hand in hand!—Did one but know!

Carl Sandburg

I cannot tell you now;
    When the wind's drive and whirl
    Blow me along no longer,
    And the wind's a whisper at last—
Maybe I'll tell you then—
                some other time.

    When the rose's flash to the sunset
    Reels to the rack and the twist,
    And the rose is a red bygone,
    When the face I love is going
    And the gate to the end shall clang,
    And it's no use to beckon or say, "So long"—
Maybe I'll tell you then—
                some other time.

I never knew any more beautiful than you:
    I have hunted you under my thoughts,
    I have broken down under the wind
    And into the roses looking for you.
        I shall never find any
            greater than you.

Robert Frost

THE PASTURE

I'm going out to clean the pasture spring;
I'll only stop to rake the leaves away
(And wait to watch the water clear, I may):
I sha'n't be gone long.—You come too.

I'm going out to fetch the little calf
That's standing by the mother. It's so young,
It totters when she licks it with her tongue.
I sha'n't be gone long.—You come too.

MEETING AND PASSING

As I went down the hill along the wall
There was a gate I had leaned at for the view
And had just turned from when I first saw you
As you came up the hill. We met. But all
We did that day was mingle great and small
Footprints in summer dust as if we drew
The figure of our being less than two
But more than one as yet. Your parasol

Pointed the decimal off with one deep thrust.
And all the time we talked you seemed to see
Something down there to smile at in the dust.
(Oh, it was without prejudice to me!)
Afterward I went past what you had passed
Before we met and you what I had passed.

TO CELIA

Drink to me only with thine eyes,
    And I will pledge with mine;
Or leave a kiss but in the cup
    And I'll not look for wine.
The thirst that from the soul doth rise
    Doth ask a drink divine;
But might I of Jove's nectar sup,
    I would not change for thine.

I sent thee late a rosy wreath,
    Not so much honouring thee
As giving it a hope that there
    It could not wither'd be;
But thou thereon didst only breathe,
    And sent'st it back to me;
Since when it grows, and smells, I swear,
    Not of itself but thee!

Wild Nights and Summer's Days

JOY

Let a joy keep you.
Reach out your hands
And take it when it runs by,
As the Apache dancer
Clutches his woman.
I have seen them
Live long and laugh loud,
Sent on singing, singing,
Smashed to the heart
Under the ribs
With a terrible love.
Joy always,
Joy everywhere—
Let joy kill you!
Keep away from the little deaths.

William Shakespeare

How oft, when thou, my music, music play'st
Upon that blessèd wood whose motion sounds
With thy sweet fingers when thou gently sway'st
The wiry concord that mine ear confounds,
Do I envy those jacks that nimble leap
To kiss the tender inward of thy hand
Whilst my poor lips, which should that harvest reap,
At the wood's boldness by thee blushing stand!
To be so tickled they would change their state
And situation with those dancing chips
O'er whom thy fingers walk with gentle gait,
Making dead wood more blessed than living lips.
   Since saucy jacks so happy are in this,
   Give them thy fingers, me thy lips to kiss.

Emily Dickinson

APOTHEOSIS

Come slowly, Eden!
Lips unused to thee,
Bashful, sip thy jasmines,
As the fainting bee,

Reaching late his flower,
Round her chamber hums,
Counts his nectars—enters,
And is lost in balms!

John Donne

Come, Madam, come, all rest my powers defie,
Until I labour, I in labour lie.
The foe oft-times having the foe in sight,
Is tir'd with standing though he never fight.
Off with that girdle, like heavens Zone glistering,
But a far fairer world incompassing.
Unpin that spangled breastplate which you wear,
That th'eyes of busie fooles may be stopt there.
Unlace your self, for that harmonious chyme,
Tells me from you, that now it is bed time.
Off with that happy busk, which I envie,
That still can be, and still can stand so nigh.
Your gown going off, such beautious state reveals,
As when from flowry meads th'hills shadow steales.
Off with that wyerie Coronet and shew
The haiery Diademe which on you doth grow:
Now off with those shooes, and then safely tread
In this loves hallow'd temple, this soft bed.

In such white robes, heaven's Angels us'd to be
Receavd by men; Thou Angel bringst with thee
A heaven like Mahomets Paradice; and though
Ill spirits walk in white, we easly know,
By this these Angels from an evil sprite,
Those set our hairs, but these out flesh upright.

 Licence my roaving hands, and let them go,
Before, behind, between, above, below.
O my America! my new-found-land,
My kingdome, safeliest when with one man man'd,
My Myne of precious stones, My Emperie,
How blest am I in this discovering thee!
To enter in these bonds, is to be free;
Then where my hand is set, my seal shall be.

 Full nakedness! All joyes are due to thee,
As souls unbodied, bodies uncloth'd must be,
To taste whole joyes. Gems which you women use
Are like Atlanta's balls, cast in mens views,
That when a fools eye lighteth on a Gem,
His earthly soul may covet theirs, not them.

Like pictures, or like books gay coverings made
For lay-men, are all women thus array'd;
Themselves are mystick books, which only wee
(Whom their imputed grace will dignifie)
Must see reveal'd. Then since that I may know;
As liberally, as to a Midwife, shew
Thy self: cast all, yea, this white lynnen hence,
[Here] is no pennance, much less innocence.

　　To teach thee, I am naked first; why then
What needst thou have more covering than a man.

Emily Dickinson

Wild nights! Wild nights!
Were I with thee,
Wild nights should be
Our luxury!

Futile the winds
To a heart in port,—
Done with the compass,
Done with the chart.

Rowing in Eden!
Ah! the sea!
Might I but moor
To-night in thee!

William Shakespeare

Take all my loves, my love, yea, take them all:
What hast thou then more than thou hadst before?
No love, my love, that thou mayst true love call—
All mine was thine before thou hadst this more.
Then if for my love thou my love receivest,
I cannot blame thee for my love thou usest;
But yet be blamed if thou this self deceivest
By wilful taste of what thyself refusest.
I do forgive thy robb'ry, gentle thief,
Although thou steal thee all my poverty;
And yet love knows it is a greater grief
To bear love's wrong than hate's known injury.
  Lascivious grace, in whom all ill well shows,
  Kill me with spites, yet we must not be foes.

William Shakespeare

Shall I compare thee to a summer's day?
Thou art more lovely and more temperate:
Rough winds do shake the darling buds of May,
And summer's lease hath all too short a date:
Sometime too hot the eye of heaven shines,
And often is his gold complexion dimm'd;
And every fair from fair sometime declines,
By chance, or nature's changing course, untrimm'd;
But thy eternal summer shall not fade,
Nor lose possession of that fair thou owest;
Nor shall Death brag thou wander'st in his shade,
When in eternal lines to time thou growest;

    So long as men can breathe, or eyes can see,
    So long lives this, and this gives life to thee.

QUESTIONS

Emily Dickinson

I've got an arrow here;
    Loving the hand that sent it,
I the dart revere.

Fell, they will say, in 'skirmish'!
    Vanquished, my soul will know,
By but a simple arrow
    Sped by an archer's bow.

Ellen Mary Patrick Downing

WERE I BUT HIS OWN WIFE

Were I but his own wife, to guard and to guide him,
    'Tis little of sorrow should fall on my dear;
I'd chant my low love-verses, stealing beside him,
    So faint and so tender his heart would but hear;
I'd pull the wild blossoms from valley and highland,
    And there at his feet I would lay them all down;
I'd sing him the songs of our poor stricken island,
    Till his heart was on fire with a love like my own.

There's a rose by his dwelling,—I'd tend the
lone treasure,
    That he might have flowers when the summer
    would come;
There's a harp in his hall,—I would wake its sweet measure,
    For he must have music to brighten his home.
Were I but his own wife, to guide and to guard him,
    'Tis little of sorrow should fall on my dear;
For every kind glance my whole life would award him,
    In sickness I'd soothe and in sadness I'd cheer.

My heart is a fount welling upward forever!
    When I think of my true-love, by night or by day,
That heart keeps its faith like a fast-flowing river
    Which gushes forever and sings on its way.
I have thoughts full of peace for his soul to repose in,
    Were I but his own wife, to win and to woo;
O sweet, if the night of misfortune were closing,
    To rise like the morning star, darling, for you!

Edgar Allan Poe

SERENADE

So sweet the hour, so calm the time,
I feel it more than half a crime,
When Nature sleeps and stars are mute,
To mar the silence ev'n with lute.
At rest on ocean's brilliant dyes
An image of Elysium lies:
Seven Pleiades entranced in Heaven,
Form in the deep another seven:
Endymion nodding from above
Sees in the sea a second love.
Within the valleys dim and brown,
And on the spectral mountain's crown,
The wearied light is dying down,
And earth, and stars, and sea, and sky
Are redolent of sleep, as I
Am redolent of thee and thine
Enthralling love, my Adeline.

But list, O list,—so soft and low
Thy lover's voice tonight shall flow,
That, scarce awake, thy soul shall deem
My words the music of a dream.
Thus, while no single sound too rude
Upon thy slumber shall intrude,
Our thoughts, our souls—O God above!
In every deed shall mingle, love.

Adelaide Anne Procter

A WOMAN'S QUESTION

Before I trust my fate to thee,
    Or place my hand in thine,
Before I let thy future give
    Color and form to mine,
Before I peril all for thee, question thy soul
    to-night for me.

I break all slighter bonds, nor feel
    A shadow of regret:
Is there one link within the Past
    That holds thy spirit yet?
Or is thy faith as clear and free as that which I can
    pledge to thee?

Does there within thy dimmest dreams
    A possible future shine,
Wherein thy life could henceforth breathe,
    Untouch'd, unshar'd by mine?
If so, at any pain or cost, O, tell me before all is lost.

Look deeper still. If thou canst feel,
    Within thy inmost soul,
That thou hast kept a portion back,
    While I have stak'd the whole;
Let no false pity spare the blow, but in true mercy tell me so.

Is there within thy heart a need
    That mine cannot fulfill?
One chord that any other hand
    Could better wake or still?
Speak now—lest at some future day my whole life
    wither and decay.

Lives there within thy nature hid
    The demon-spirit Change,
Shedding a passing glory still
    On all things new and strange?
It may not be thy fault alone—but shield my heart
    against thy own.

Couldst thou withdraw thy hand one day
    And answer to my claim,
That Fate, and that to-day's mistake—
    Not thou—had been to blame?
Some soothe their conscience thus; but thou wilt surely
    warn and save me now.

Nay, answer not,—I dare not hear,
    The words would come too late;
Yet I would spare thee all remorse,
    So, comfort thee, my fate—
Whatever on my heart may fall—remember,
    I would risk it all!

Carl Sandburg

On the breakwater in the summer dark, a man and a girl
   are sitting
She across his knee and they are looking face into face
Talking to each other without words, singing rhythms in
   silence to each other.
A funnel of white ranges the blue dusk from an
   outgoing boat
Playing its searchlight, puzzled, abrupt, over a
   streak of green
And two on the breakwater keep their silence,
   she on his knee.

O never say that I was false of heart,
Though absence seemed my flame to qualify—
As easy might I from myself depart
As from my soul, which in thy breast doth lie.
That is my home of love. If I have ranged,
Like him that travels I return again,
Just to the time, not with the time exchanged,
So that myself bring water for my stain.
Never believe, though in my nature reigned
All frailties that besiege all kinds of blood,
That it could so preposterously be stained
To leave for nothing all thy sum of good;

   For nothing this wide universe I call
   Save thou my rose; in it thou art my all.

William Shakespeare

So are you to my thoughts as food to life,
Or as sweet-seasoned showers are to the ground;
And for the peace of you I hold such strife
As 'twixt a miser and his wealth is found:
Now proud as an enjoyer, and anon
Doubting the filching age will steal his treasure;
Now counting best to be with you alone,
Then bettered that the world may see my pleasure;
Sometime all full with feasting on your sight,
And by and by clean starvèd for a look;
Possessing or pursuing no delight
Save what is had or must from you be took.

    Thus do I pine and surfeit day by day,
    Or gluttoning on all, or all away.

Alter? When the hills do.
Falter? When the sun
Question if his glory
Be the perfect one.

Surfeit? When the daffodil
Doth of the dew:
Even as herself, O friend!
I will of you!

LONGINGS

James Joyce

CHAMBER MUSIC

The twilight turns from amethyst
    To deep and deeper blue,
The lamp fills with a pale green glow
    The trees of the avenue.

The old piano plays an air,
    Sedate and slow and gay;
She bends upon the yellow keys,
    Her head inclines this way.

Shy thoughts and grave wide eyes and hands
    That wander as they list—
The twilight turns to darker blue
    With lights of amethyst.

William Butler Yeats

THE FALLING OF THE LEAVES

Autumn is over the long leaves that love us,
And over the mice in the barley sheaves;
Yellow the leaves of the rowan above us,
And yellow the wet wild-strawberry leaves.

The hour of the waning of love has beset us,
And weary and worn are our sad souls now;
Let us part, ere the season of passion forget us,
With a kiss and a tear on thy drooping brow.

William Butler Yeats

DOWN BY THE SALLEY GARDENS

Down by the salley gardens my love and I did meet;
She passed the salley gardens with little snow-white feet.
She bid me take love easy, as the leaves grow on the tree;
But I, being young and foolish, with her would not agree.

In a field by the river my love and I did stand,
And on my leaning shoulder she laid her snow-white hand.
She bid me take life easy, as the grass grows on the weirs;
But I was young and foolish, and now am full of tears.

William Butler Yeats

The Heart of the Woman

O what to me the little room
That was brimmed up with prayer and rest;
He bade me out into the gloom,
And my breast lies upon his breast.

O what to me my mother's care,
The house where I was safe and warm;
The shadowy blossom of my hair
Will hide us from the bitter storm.

O hiding hair and dewy eyes,
I am no more with life and death,
My heart upon his warm heart lies,
My breath is mixed into his breath.

William Butler Yeats

I went out to the hazel wood,
Because a fire was in my head,
And cut and peeled a hazel wand,
And hooked a berry to a thread;
And when white moths were on the wing,
And moth-like stars were flickering out,
I dropped the berry in a stream
And caught a little silver trout.

When I had laid it on the floor
I went to blow the fire a-flame,
But something rustled on the floor,
And someone called me by my name:
It had become a glimmering girl
With apple blossom in her hair
Who called me by my name and ran
And faded through the brightening air.

Though I am old with wandering
Through hollow lands and hilly lands,
I will find out where she has gone,
And kiss her lips and take her hands;
And walk among long dappled grass,
And pluck till time and times are done
The silver apples of the moon,
The golden apples of the sun.

DREAMS

Carl Sandburg

The monotone of the rain is beautiful,
And the sudden rise and slow relapse
Of the long multitudinous rain.

The sun on the hills is beautiful,
Or a captured sunset sea-flung,
Bannered with fire and gold.

A face I know is beautiful—
With fire and gold of sky and sea,
And the peace of long warm rain.

DREAM GIRL

You will come one day in a waver of love,
Tender as dew, impetuous as rain,
The tan of the sun will be on your skin,
The purr of the breeze in your murmuring speech,
You will pose with a hill-flower grace.

You will come, with your slim, expressive arms,
A poise of the head no sculptor has caught
And nuances spoken with shoulder and neck,
Your face in a pass-and-repass of moods
As many as skies in delicate change
Of cloud and blue and flimmering sun.

Yet,
You may not come, O girl of a dream,
We may but pass as the world goes by
And take from a look of eyes into eyes,
A film of hope and a memoried day.

I have no life but this,
To lead it here;
Nor any death, but lest
Dispelled from there;

Nor tie to earths to come,
Nor action new,
Except through this extent,
The realm of you.

WHITE SHOULDERS

Your white shoulders
   I remember
And your shrug of laughter.

   Low laughter
   Shaken slow
From your white shoulders.

William Butler Yeats

The quarrel of the sparrows in the eaves,
The full round moon and the star-laden sky,
And the loud song of the ever-singing leaves,
Had hid away earth's old and weary cry.

And then you came with those red mournful lips,
And with you came the whole of the world's tears
And all the trouble of her labouring ships,
And all the trouble of her myriad years.

And now the sparrows warring in the eaves,
The curd-pale moon, the white stars in the sky,
And the loud chaunting of the unquiet leaves,
Are shaken with earth's old and weary cry.

Emily Dickinson

WITH A FLOWER

I hide myself within my flower,
That wearing on your breast,
You, unsuspecting, wear me too—
And angels know the rest.

I hide myself within my flower,
That, fading from your vase,
You, unsuspecting, feel for me
Almost a loneliness.

When in the chronicle of wasted time
I see descriptions of the fairest wights,
And beauty making beautiful old rhyme
In praise of ladies dead and lovely knights;
Then in the blazon of sweet beauty's best,
Of hand, of foot, of lip, of eye, of brow,
I see their antique pen would have expressed
Ev'n such a beauty as you master now.
So all their praises are but prophecies
Of this our time, all you prefiguring,
And for they looked but with divining eyes
They had not skill enough your worth to sing;
    For we which now behold these present days
    Have eyes to wonder, but lack tongues to praise.

MESSAGES

Robert Frost

THE TELEPHONE

"When I was just as far as I could walk
From here to-day,
There was an hour
All still
When leaning with my head against a flower
I heard you talk.
Don't say I didn't, for I heard you say—
You spoke from that flower on the window sill—
Do you remember what it was you said?"

"First tell me what it was you thought you heard."

"Having found the flower and driven a bee away,
I leaned my head,
And holding by the stalk,
I listened and I thought I caught the word—
What was it? Did you call me by my name?
Or did you say—
Someone said 'Come'—I heard it as I bowed."

"I may have thought as much, but not aloud."

"Well, so I came."

Emily Dickinson

THE LETTER

"Going to him! Happy letter! Tell him—
Tell him the page I didn't write;
Tell him I only said the syntax,
And left the verb and the pronoun out.
Tell him just how the fingers hurried,
Then how they waded, slow, slow, slow;
And then you wished you had eyes in your pages,
So you could see what moved them so.

"Tell him it wasn't a practised writer,
You guessed, from the way the sentence toiled;
You could hear the bodice tug, behind you,
As if it held but the might of a child;
You almost pitied it, you, it worked so.
Tell him—No, you may quibble there,
For it would split his heart to know it,
And then you and I were silenter.

"Tell him night finished before we finished,
And the old clock kept neighing 'day!'
And you got sleepy and begged to be ended—
What could it hinder so, to say?
Tell him just how she sealed you, cautious,
But if he ask where you are hid
Until to-morrow,—happy letter!
Gesture, coquette, and shake your head!"

Heloise

I have your picture in my room; I never pass it without stopping to look at it; and yet when you are present with me I scarce ever cast my eyes on it. If a picture, which is but a mute representation of an object, can give such pleasure, what cannot letters inspire? They have souls; they can speak; they have in them all that force which expresses the transports of the heart; they have all the fire of our passions, they can raise them as much as if the persons themselves were present; they have all the tenderness and the delicacy of speech, and sometimes even the boldness of expression beyond it.

We may write to each other; so innocent a pleasure is not denied us. Let us not lose through negligence the only happiness which is left us, and the only one perhaps which the malice of our enemies can never ravish from us. I shall read that you are my husband and you shall see me sign myself your wife. In spite of all our misfortunes you may be what you please in your letter.

Letters were first invented for consoling such solitary wretches as myself. Having lost the substantial pleasures of seeing and possessing you, I shall in some measure compensate this loss by the satisfaction I shall find in your writing. There I shall read your most sacred thoughts; I shall carry them always about with me, I shall kiss them every moment; if you can be capable of any jealousy let it be for the fond caresses I shall bestow upon your letters, and envy only the happiness of those rivals.

A LATE WALK

When I go up through the mowing field,
    The headless aftermath,
Smooth-laid like thatch with the heavy dew,
    Half closes the garden path.

And when I come to the garden ground,
    The whir of sober birds
Up from the tangle of withered weeds
    Is sadder than any words.

A tree beside the wall stands bare,
    But a leaf that lingered brown,
Disturbed, I doubt not, by my thought,
    Comes softly rattling down.

I end not far from my going forth
    By picking the faded blue
Of the last remaining aster flower
    To carry again to you.

William Butler Yeats

THE PITY OF LOVE

A pity beyond all telling
Is hid in the heart of love:
The folk who are buying and selling
The clouds on their journey above
The cold wet winds ever blowing
And the shadowy hazel grove
Where mouse-gray waters are flowing
Threaten the head that I love.

If you were coming in the fall,
I'd brush the summer by
With half a smile and half a spurn,
As housewives do a fly.

If I could see you in a year,
I'd wind the months in balls,
And put them each in separate drawers,
For fear their numbers fuse.

If only centuries delayed,
I'd count them on my hand,
Subtracting till my fingers dropped
Into Van Diemen's land.

If certain, when this life was out,
That yours and mine should be,
I'd toss it yonder like a rind,
And take eternity.

But now, uncertain of the length
Of this that is between,
It goads me, like the goblin bee,
That will not state its sting.

William Shakespeare

That time of year thou mayst in me behold
When yellow leaves, or none, or few, do hang
Upon those boughs which shake against the cold,
Bare ruined choirs where late the sweet birds sang.
In me thou seest the twilight of such day
As after sunset fadeth in the west,
Which by and by black night doth take away,
Death's second self, that seals up all in rest.
In me thou seest the glowing of such fire
That on the ashes of his youth doth lie
As the death-bed whereon it must expire,
Consumed with that which it was nourished by.
This thou perceiv'st, which makes thy love more strong,
To love that well which thou must leave ere long.

LOSSES

Emily Dickinson

I cannot live with you,
It would be life,
And life is over there
Behind the shelf

The sexton keeps the key to,
Putting up
Our life, his porcelain,
Like a cup

Discarded of the housewife,
Quaint or broken;
A newer Sèvres pleases,
Old ones crack.

I could not die with you,
For one must wait
To shut the other's gaze down,—
You could not.

And I, could I stand by
And see you freeze,

Without my right of frost,
Death's privilege?

Nor could I rise with you,
Because your face
Would put out Jesus',
That new grace

Glow plain and foreign
On my homesick eye,
Except that you, than he
Shone closer by.

They'd judge us—how?
For you served Heaven, you know,
Or sought to;
I could not,

Because you saturated sight,
And I had no more eyes
For sordid excellence
As Paradise.

And were you lost, I would be,
Though my name
Rang loudest
On the heavenly fame.

And were you saved,
And I condemned to be
Where you were not,
That self were hell to me.

So we must keep apart,
You there, I here,
With just the door ajar
That oceans are,
And prayer,
And that pale sustenance,
Despair!

Carl Sandburg

LOSSES

I have love
And a child,
A banjo
And shadows.
(Losses of God,
All will go
And one day
We will hold
Only the shadows.)

Emily Dickinson

THE CONTRACT

I gave myself to him,
And took himself for pay.
The solemn contract of a life
Was ratified this way.

The wealth might disappoint,
Myself a poorer prove
Than this great purchaser suspect:
The daily own of Love

Depreciates the vision;
But, till the merchant buy,
Still fable, in the isles of spice,
The subtle cargoes lie.

At least, 't is mutual risk,—
Some found it mutual gain;
Sweet debt of Life,—each night to owe,
Insolvent, every noon.

Emily Dickinson

CONSECRATION

Proud of my broken heart since thou didst break it,
    Proud of the pain I did not feel till thee,
Proud of my night since thou with moons dost slake it,
    Not to partake thy passion, my humility.

Carl Sandburg

Memory of you is . . . a blue spear of flower.
I cannot remember the name of it.
Alongside a bold dripping poppy is fire and silk.
And they cover you.

William Shakespeare

When, in disgrace with fortune and men's eyes,
I all alone beweep my outcast state,
And trouble deaf heaven with my bootless cries,
And look upon myself and curse my fate,
Wishing me like to one more rich in hope,
Featured like him, like him with friends possessed,
Desiring this man's art and that man's scope,
With what I most enjoy contented least:
Yet in these thoughts myself almost despising,
Haply I think on thee, and then my state,
Like to the lark at break of day arising
From sullen earth, sings hymns at heaven's gate;
　　For thy sweet love remembered such wealth brings
　　That then I scorn to change my state with kings'.

EPHEMERA

Elizabeth Tollet

Ask me no more my truth to prove,
What I would suffer for my love;
With thee I would in exile go
To regions of eternal snow;
O'er floods by solid ice confin'd,
Through forests bare, with northern wind;
While all around my eyes I cast,
Where all is wild, and all is waste.
If there the timorous stag you chase,
Or rouse to fight a fiercer race,
Undaunted, I thy arms would bear,
And give thy hand the hunter's spear.
When the low sun withdraws his light,
And menaces an half-year's night,
The conscious moon and stars above
Shall guide me with my wandering love.
Beneath the mountain's hollow brow,
Or in its rocky cells below,
Thy rural feast I would provide,
Nor envy palaces their pride;

The softest moss should dress thy bed,
With savage spoils about thee spread;
Whilst faithful love the watch should keep,
To banish danger from thy sleep.

William Shakespeare

My mistress' eyes are nothing like the sun;
Coral is far more red than her lips' red.
If snow be white, why then her breasts are dun;
If hairs be wires, black wires grow on her head.
I have seen roses damasked, red and white,
But no such roses see I in her cheeks;
And in some perfumes is there more delight
Than in the breath that from my mistress reeks.
I love to hear her speak, yet well I know
That music hath a far more pleasing sound.
I grant I never saw a goddess go:
My mistress when she walks treads on the ground.
  And yet, by heaven, I think my love as rare
  As any she belied with false compare.

William Shakespeare

How like a winter hath my absence been
From thee, the pleasure of the fleeting year!
What freezings have I felt, what dark days seen,
What old December's bareness everywhere!
And yet this time removed was summer's time,
The teeming autumn big with rich increase,
Bearing the wanton burden of the prime
Like widowed wombs after their lord's decease.
Yet this abundant issue seemed to me
But hope of orphans and unfathered fruit,
For summer and his pleasures wait on thee,
And thou away, the very birds are mute;

    Or if they sing, 'tis with so dull a cheer
    That leaves look pale, dreading the winter's near.

William Blake

LOVE'S SECRET

Never seek to tell thy love,
　　Love that never told can be;
For the gentle wind doth move
　　Silently, invisibly.

I told my love, I told my love,
　　I told her all my heart,
Trembling, cold, in ghastly fears.
　　Ah! she did depart!

Soon after she was gone from me,
　　A traveller came by,
Silently, invisibly:
　　He took her with a sigh.

Emily Dickinson

Heart, we will forget him!
    You and I, to-night!
You may forget the warmth he gave,
    I will forget the light.

When you have done, pray tell me,
    That I may straight begin;
Haste! lest while you're lagging,
    I remember him!

William Butler Yeats

"Your eyes that once were never weary of mine
"Are bowed in sorrow under pendulous lids,
"Because our love is waning."

And then she:
"Although our love is waning, let us stand
"By the lone border of the lake once more,
"Together in that hour of gentleness
"When the poor tired child, Passion, falls asleep:
"How far away the stars seem, and how far
"Is our first kiss, and ah, how old my heart!"

Pensive they paced along the faded leaves,
While slowly he whose hand held hers replied:
"Passion has often worn our wandering hearts."

The woods were round them, and the yellow leaves
Fell like faint meteors in the gloom, and once
A rabbit old and lame limped down the path;
Autumn was over him: and now they stood
On the lone border of the lake once more:

Turning, he saw that she had thrust dead leaves
Gathered in silence, dewy as her eyes,
In bosom and hair.

"Ah, do not mourn," he said,
"That we are tired, for other loves await us;
"Hate on and love through unrepining hours.
"Before us lies eternity; our souls
"Are love, and a continual farewell."

Emily Dickinson

BEQUEST

> You left me, sweet, two legacies,—
> A legacy of love
> A Heavenly Father would content,
> Had He the offer of;
>
> You left me boundaries of pain
> Capacious as the sea,
> Between eternity and time,
> Your consciousness and me.

Emily Dickinson

THE LOST JEWEL

> I held a jewel in my fingers
> And went to sleep.
> The day was warm, and the winds were prosy;
> I said: "'T will keep."
>
> I woke and chid my honest fingers,—
> The gem was gone;
> And now an amethyst remembrance
> Is all I own.

William Blake

I went to the Garden of Love,
And saw what I never had seen:
A Chapel was built in the midst,
Where I used to play on the green.

And the gates of this Chapel were shut,
And "Thou shalt not" writ over the door;
So I turn'd to the Garden of Love
That so many sweet flowers bore;

And I saw it was filled with graves,
And tomb-stones where flowers should be;
And Priests in black gowns were walking their rounds,
And binding with briars my joys & desires.

Lord Byron

So, we'll go no more a-roving
  So late into the night,
Though the heart be still as loving.
  And the moon be still as bright.

For the sword outwears its sheath,
  And the soul wears out the breast,
And the heart must pause to breathe,
  And love itself have rest.

Though the night was made for loving,
  And the day returns too soon,
Yet, we'll go no more a-roving
  By the light of the moon.

William Shakespeare

To me, fair friend, you never can be old;
For as you were when first your eye I eyed,
Such seems your beauty still. Three winters cold
Have from the forests shook three summers' pride;
Three beauteous springs to yellow autumn turned
In process of the seasons have I seen,
Three April perfumes in three hot Junes burned
Since first I saw you fresh, which yet are green.
Ah yet doth beauty, like a dial hand,
Steal from his figure and no pace perceived;
So your sweet hue, which methinks still doth stand,
Hath motion, and mine eye may be deceived.
    For fear of which, hear this, thou age unbred:
    Ere you were born was beauty's summer dead.

William Butler Yeats

When you are old and gray and full of sleep,
And nodding by the fire, take down this book,
And slowly read, and dream of the soft look
Your eyes had once, and of their shadows deep;

How many loved your moments of glad grace,
And loved your beauty with love false or true;
But one man loved the pilgrim soul in you,
And loved the sorrows of your changing face.

And bending down beside the glowing bars
Murmur, a little sadly, how love fled
And paced upon the mountains overhead
And hid his face amid a crowd of stars.